# Sexual Manners in the XXI Century

A Self Help book by Marcellux Bosq.

# Sexual Manners in the XXI Century

✦

## Redefining the rules of etiquette for a proper sex in our actual society

*A self help book for those people who want to do certain things with charm*

## Marcellux Bosq

iUniverse, Inc.
New York  Lincoln  Shanghai

# Sexual Manners in the XXI Century
## Redefining the rules of etiquette for a proper sex in our actual society

iUniverse, Inc.

For information address:
iUniverse, Inc.
2021 Pine Lake Road, Suite 100
Lincoln, NE 68512
www.iuniverse.com

Images and Illustrations by Marcellux Bosq

ISBN: 0-595-27683-0

Printed in the United States of America

To Lucy, the one whose mind was in the sky and used a diamond.

*Think you I am no stronger than my sex...*

—William Shakespeare

# Contents

# Other works from the Author

(You've got a summary resume of the author at the end of this book)

## Books

### From Self-Help Serial
*The Inner Warrior:* A practical guide to fight against our fears and to conquer a higher level of existence

### From Self-Entertainment Serial
*Shakespeare's Thematic Puzzles!:* Includes crossword puzzles, riddles and word search games inspired in the plays of the bard, for your fun and entertainment.
*Thematic Puzzles!:* Crossword & Word Search puzzles. Includes puzzles about motion pictures, actors, music, writers, Internet, books, American Presidents, computers…etc.

### From Science & Technology Serial
*Understanding 99% of Artificial Neural Networks:* Introduction & Tricks
*Programming a REAL Internet Site with ASP & HTML.*

## Images, Paintings and Sculptures
The author's visual arts page can be found at http://marcellux.tripod.com.
Here you'll find the paintings that were used as covers of the books and some free gifts to visitors as Calendars, Bookplates and Seasons' Greetings cards.

# *Foreword*

This book is NOT related to any religion nor sect. The no believing people will not find contents that could induce them to profess any special faith nor adhering to a sect. However, I don't know exactly why, but the great monotheists religions use to spend much time talking about what it is proper or not to do at bedrooms. Then, I must suppose that if I start to talk about these matters with a different vision, some of them would think that I am doing something that is related to them, something that THEY must do (and not me). Let me tell you, in advance, that the intention of this book is to bring light to people, the light of knowledge, and this can't be something wrong. In summary: This book is not adequate for fanatics.

If you think you know all you have to know about sex, and that nothing else is necessary to be known, well…This book is not for you.

# Preface

✦

## Is this book for me?

This book was made for:

- Gentlemen
- Ladies
- Men who would like to behave like gentleman, but don't know how to do it.
- Women who'd like to behave like ladies, but don't know how to do it.
- People interested in manners
- People curious about all the matters related to sex.

If you can identify yourself with some of these characteristics, you are one of the people who can find help in this book. Welcome

# Acknowledgements

This book is part of a serial of self help books that were born as an Internet site. **The page of Marcellux Bosq** was published on the net as a way to communicate with other people with similar interests. Due to its success, it came to light the idea of making a book inspired in it. Soon, the book became a serial. It was then, inspired by the readers. Thanks to all of them.

This work is dedicated to those people who need to change their attitudes toward life and require a bit of help to be able to make it. Read the ethics and policies at the foreword section.

# List of Abbreviations and Glossary

**Sex:**

- Definition 1) One of the principal problems that mankind has got since the beginning of times.

- Definition 2) The eldest problem of them all.

- Definition 3) What would we do without it?

- Definition 4) Something to talk about at the hairdresser's with our friends.

- Definition 5) Something we suspect the others do better and more frequently than us.

- Definition 6) What was that? I've heard about it…

**Manners:**

- Definition 1) Something that many people talk about without knowing what it is.

- Definition 2) Good manners are what your mother told you to do when you were young (or perhaps yesterday morning…)

**Self Help:**

It is the help or advice that people can learn from a book, a video a TV program or any other way in order to improve the quality of their lives. It is not a medical treatment given by a doctor in a hospital . To know about the proper manners to perform a task is one of the best uses you can give to self help because it teaches you what are the others expecting form you.

**Q-life:**

Quality of Life: You improve your quality of life when you have good sex.

# Introduction

○ ○ ○ ○ ○ ○ ○ ○ ○ ○ ○ ○ ○ ○ ○ ○ ○ ○ ○ ○ ○ ○ ○ ○ ○ ○ ○ ○ ○ ○ ○ ○ ○

*Bring me a lock. Chain me to my lover, and leave us alone; forever…*

## Introduction:

This book is about sex. Our own sex. Sex is a problem: The problem to get more sex.

In the stone age, people used to solve this problem using the easy way. If you were a man looking for an intercourse, you just had to "go hunting"(hunting a girl, of course!).

Suppose you are Mr. Fred Cavernman and you are looking for your fiancée. (She still doesn't know she is your fiancée, but these tiny aspects of the relationship doesn't matter at all). All you have to do is to walk in the prairie with your big stick until you see a girl. It only takes a small punch, and VOILA!: the girl is yours…(she is knocked out, but she is yours, all yours)

The girl used to awake in your cave, just to notice she was officially married (with you). Nothing else was needed.

Perhaps some inquisitive reader may be wondering about her feelings…Feelings? What was that?

Oh, how simple were those idyllic days!

You didn't have to ask the opinion of your friends about your boyfriend, you didn't have to ask your parents for permission if you were under 18!. (And of course, nobody used to marry just to leave their parent's cave)

However, the best of all was this: There was no AIDS at that time! We haven't invented it yet!

As I said before, life was a paradise in the stone age…

However, all that glisters is not gold.[1]

Time went by, and we evolved as human beings and society until the present. (—*"Really? Who was the fool who said that?"*—My aunty used to say).

Well, the fact is that the relationships between the sexes started to be more complicated, and more, and more…until now.

Dark Ages, Romanticism, Victorian times, Sexual Revolution of the 1960's…We are living in a word that has changed its points of view dramatically about sex.

However, there is something that every age in the history of the world had: Manners. Good manners, bad manners, improper behavior and lack of sensibility are characteristics of all human society.

We, men and women of the XXI century are not exceptions to this rule.

There was always an appropriate way to talk to a lady, and also an appropriate way to ask her to go to the bedroom with you.

It is said that the difference between a gentleman and a beggar is not his fortune, but his manners. We can find the same difference between a lady and a street walker…

This book was written for those men who want to behave as gentlemen in the most intimate moments, and for those women who want to be treated as ladies, even when they are wearing nothing at all.

---

1.    By the way: I love to make quotes from Shakespeare, excuse me

# PART I
## Excuses from a sinner

# 1

## *I don't know exactly why, but I feel guilty when I talk about sex*

○ ○ ○ ○ ○ ○ ○ ○ ○ ○ ○ ○ ○ ○ ○ ○ ○ ○ ○ ○ ○ ○ ○ ○ ○ ○ ○ ○ ○ ○ ○ ○ ○ ○

*"Even though many people have got the means to solve their problems by themselves, they do not use them, and they remain suffering and frustrated"*

## Guilt and Sex

Manners are related to the behavior that is accepted in a society in a particular moment of its history. This means that there is not a fixed set of rules that may be practical forever, or for everybody. The world has historically been divided between the Western and Eastern cultures. Each one of them has a different point of view about the attitudes that people should have in a determinate moment. As the author of this book belongs to the Western Culture, this will be the point of view that will be predominant in this work. As a mater of fact, I'd like to comment that you "belong" to your culture. There's nothing you can do about it. If you were born in England, and you go to live to China, you are an English man in Asia, not a Chinese citizen.

So, this book will show the feelings and beliefs of men and women in any of the countries that conform the Western Hemisphere (or the western culture, as you prefer).

As we were saying, manners are related to culture, (the same as sex) so if we want to speak about them, we have to speak a bit about our culture.

In our western scale of values, guilt is the predominant and most important factor that must be taken into account.

We can say that 90% of our population has a Catholic, Protestant, Jewish or Muslim origin.

This remains a problem when we want to generalize the themes, because each religion has its own rules of behavior.

The most important thing we have to say here is that this is a book of manners, not a book of moral.

Morality is a concept that is related to religions. For example, for some Islamic women, the standard proper garment they must use is a black dress that covers all their bodies and a veil. It is immoral for them to use mini skirts.

So, we must have in clear that the expressions that are said in this book could be in collision with some of the precepts that religions teach.

However, it is not the purpose of the author to offend anyone. The fact is that actual manners are sometimes in collision with those postulates. This is not the right place to discuss about society and religion. We will only concentrate here in the norms of behavior that are related to the proper way we have to act in the process of seduction and romance. That's all.

# Lessons extracted from Chapter one:

- Manners are the behaviors that are accepted in a society in a particular moment of its history.

- This is a book of manners, not a book of moral.

- Actual manners are sometimes in collision with moral postulates.

- So, we must have in clear that the expressions that are said in this book could be in collision with some of the precepts that religions teach. (As the one that says that marriage is just to have children and not to enjoy sex)

# PART II

## The first approaching to love

# 2

## *About gentlemen, ladies, truck drivers and street walkers.*

o o o o o o o o o o o o o o o o o o o o o o o o o o o o o o o o o o o
*Success is just the last step of a ladder of failures…(Marcellux)*

### What you do makes you who you are:

What are manners? What is a proper behavior?. All of us are social beings in a social world. In a way or another, we want to have our place in it. Some people are trend setters: All the others copy what they do (However, you have to be famous to be a trend setter). Some others are revolutionaries: They go against the establishment, they want to change the rules. These groups do not need manners; they invent they own attitudes. One thing they've got in common is that both of them are minor groups.

As a matter of fact, ordinary people do not care about manners. It is very frequent to see people who belong to the working classes acting in a rude way. Perhaps they believe that being polite is something connected to the high society, so they think it is not for them, because they are poor.

What a lack of perception!

However, there is another minor group[1], who are the ones who consider that education is worth, and that manners should be an inherent part of the life of the modern man (and woman). I am one of them, and I assume that you, reader, are

---

1.    Yes, yes: we are a minority. We must assume that in our "modern" society, the majority of people do not care about manners.

also a member of the group. For us, there are two concepts that focus our lives: The concept of a gentleman, and the concept of a lady.

"Men" and "gentlemen" are not synonyms. Not for us. We are born as men, but only few of us deserve the honor to be called gentlemen. The same happens with women.

In this book, the figure of the "gentleman" and the "lady" will be archetypes of personality to be imitated. We will use them as metaphors of all the things that have to be done, of all the right attitudes that we have to exhibit in public, in special, in front of the other sex.

Sex, as any other human activity, has its own rituals, a proper way to do the things. This is the core matter of this book.

So, **gentleman** and **lady**, are positive words for us, the image we have to follow.

As far as I'm concerned, we can't speak about light if we don't mention the shadow; we can't speak about enlightening if we don't mention the obscurity. That's why we also need some archetypical personalities to show everything that is wrong, everything that we have to avoid.

We will use the figures of the **Truck driver** *(also called "cavern man", or "beggar")*, and the **Street walker** (or *"prostitute"*) in order to do that.

When I say beggar, I am not referring to those poor souls that are homeless, and live with dignity their circumstances. I mean those men who are rude, uneducated, and are pride of it. (it means that they do nothing to overcome this fact). Truck drivers in general act the same as beggars do. They are good workers, honest and trustable persons, but they are not famous for being people with good manners. So, we'll use the metaphor of the Truck driver as the opposite of the gentleman.

The same happens with the street walker (I prefer to call them this way. The word "prostitute" is perhaps too pejorative).

The principal characteristic of the cavern men and the street walker is vulgarity: Both are extremely vulgar.

## The gentleman and the lady spend their lives fighting against vulgarity.

When we talk about sex, the same concepts are applied. We have to realize that there are gentleman and ladies, but there are also cavern men and street walkers. In this field, vulgarity becomes obscenity.

## We will say that something is obscene when the fact is vulgar (or it is not aesthetic).

This word is often used in an inappropriate context, so many people have a vague idea of its real meaning. Many people think that is a kind of synonym of words like "erotic" and "dirty" (at the same time), so they use it when they want to show that some erotic behavior is dirty. Some others think that every erotic act is dirty so they just use sentences like:

*"This is obscene", or "that was obscene"*

For them, erotism is obscene. Some others say that some of the films of the Italian director Paolo Passolini are obscene…

For an educated person, art cannot be obscene by definition. Let's talk about visual arts: Is Goya's "Naked Maja" an obscene painting?. Ridiculous…

---

**In summary**: From the point of view of the sexual manners, the word "obscene" is related to vulgarity, not with the erotism itself. Only if a sexual practice is considered vulgar, we will call it obscene.

In this book, we will use four basic concepts: two positive, and two negative ones.

---

The following table shows this fact to us:

Table I

**Personalities from the point of view of the manners**

| Attitude | Men | Women |
|---|---|---|
| Imitate the | Gentleman | Lady |
| Avoid the | Cavern man/Truck Driver | Street Walker |

All this book will be based in this table.

You will be taught how to be a gentleman (or a lady).

You will be warned against the attitudes of cavern men and street walkers.

To finish this chapter, nothing better than the golden rule of the gentleman:

*You have to do nothing to be a cavern man, but it takes a big effort to become a gentleman.*

# Lessons extracted from Chapter two.

- Ordinary people do not care about manners. We will refer to them as cavern men. It is very frequent to see people who belong to the working classes acting in a rude way. However, many rich people are rude too. So, your financial statements have nothing to do with your manners.

- The ones who consider that manners should be an inherent part of the behavior of the educated men and women are called gentlemen and ladies. We will call cavern man and street walkers to those rude people that don't care about manners.

- Sex, as any other human activity, has its own rituals, a proper way to do the things. This is the core matter of this book.

- You have to do nothing to be a cavern man, but it takes a big effort to become a gentleman.

- The gentleman and the lady spend their lives fighting against vulgarity.

# 3

## *The first contacts.*

### To be a gentleman or not to be a gentleman: That is the question

Sex is not only referred to the copulation act. Animals copulate. Truck drivers copulate…This matter is not so easy for a gentleman. The first thing he has to know, is that the ceremony, the rituals that conduct to sex are as important as the act itself. We will call these ceremonies as "seduction".

---

*Seduction is an activity reserved for gentlemen and ladies only.*

---

### Beer Vs. Champagne: The difference between "Eau Perrier" and a glass of water

The seduction games between men and women are usually called "Romance". The practice of romance is a highly recommended activity for gentlemen and ladies.

Seduction is seen by ordinary men as something that "is not for them". Of course we agree: It is not for them. The refined relationship resultant from a seduction game is a concept too erudite for them to understand. A standard lady wants to be seduced in a romantic way just because she wants to be sure that the man that pretends her favors is a gentleman. If she prefers an intercourse with a truck driver full of sweat, that means she is not a lady (I think).

Remember well this: Romance is a test, where a man shows a woman he is a gentleman, and the woman shows him she is a lady. One of the easiest ways to discover the difference between the gentleman and the cavern man, is to see the way they play the game of romance.

Street walkers don't need to be seduced. They are merely driven to a place where they can have sex.

Think in a sweated truck driver trying to pick up a girl in a dirty motel of a dusty road (in the middle of nowhere)...Do you see the scene as something romantic? Can you imagine him giving her orchids? How about a drunk man coming home from the bar? Do you see him telling sweet words of love to his wife when he meets her? Of course not.

As I said before, cavern men consider the games of seduction as something worthless. Many married men have used these techniques just to marry their wives. Once they got the objective, the seduction was over. Think about all the people you know that has been married for a long time...How many of them are still using romance as a usual behavior?

Any woman who wants to behave as a proper lady shouldn't have to pay attention to a man who does not practice the arts of seduction in order to get her favors. A gentleman is an expert in them. He does it for several reasons:

a.  It is improper for a gentleman to date street walkers because he has an aversion to vulgarity. A man may have as many girlfriends as he wants (not at the same time, please), but all of them have to be ladies.

b.  A gentleman feels uncomfortable if he behaves as a cavern man. He does not drink in excess in front of a lady because it is extremely improper for a lady to see him drunken.

c.  Manners are a way of life. Sail men act like sail men. Politicians act like politicians, and construction workers act like construction workers. You don't expect a male coiffeur from Beverly Hills to act like a rude truck driver from the west coast. Well, the same applies to gentlemen. They must look and act like gentlemen.

## The first steps with a lady

Suppose you see someone of the opposite sex. You want to seduce this person. What do you have to do?

The first contact with a lady is a crucial moment. The ordinary people do not think about it. A truck driver just watches at a beautiful girl and starts to think about sex.

Think in this typical scene: A girl is going back home. Round the corner, there is a group of truck drivers. What are you expecting from them when they see her?. Of course they will start to say stupid phrases to her (as *"hey baby come with pappy"*, *or "stay with me, honey"*). Typical attitude of cavern men.

Remember this: The gentleman NEVER says stupid words to a girl in the street. A lady never pays attention to a stupid who tells her nonsense phrases in the street.

## Where to do the first contact

Some basic rules about the first contact:

- Ladies avoid contact with strangers because they just go out with gentlemen.

- Trust is the key to succeed. The lady must feel she "knows" you in some way before she accepts your proposal. A gentleman has to give her information about him before he asks her to go out with him.

- There are several ways to give a lady indirect information about a gentleman. (The way he looks, the way he acts, the people they know in common). All of these facts can (and must) be combined to create the famous "first sight" or the right attitude towards romance.

- Gentlemen only have to initiate the first contact with a lady if the circumstances are adequate. Truck drivers just "pick up girls"

- Gentlemen do not pick up whores. Casual sex with girls known in the street is not a business related to them. Let it for truck drivers.

- They don't even say nasty words to girls in the street. Truck drivers do. It is absolutely forbidden to say things like *"What a pair (of tits) you've got pussy!"*

If you look like Leonardo Di Caprio or Brad Pitt, you can go directly to any girl you want and ask her to go out with you. [1]

Unfortunately, the average gentleman is not as handsome as they are, so the first contact is harder to get, and they must use their initiative to reach the target.

In general, streets are not a good place to initiate something. Try to find a neutral place to do it. The best strategy for a proper introduction of yourself with the other person is to find someone who knows her and can introduce yourselves. This technique is extremely effective in some places as schools, universities or social clubs.

If you can't get someone to do it for you, you have another strategy. It requires a bit of intelligence tasks. You have to spy a bit the lady (or the gentleman) and find out the activities she likes. For example, if she is a member of your sports club, you may find out that she likes tennis, for example. You have to find an activity she likes to do and that you can share with her. For example, if she likes tennis (and you also play), find out if there is a local championship or tourney for men and women doubles, so you can just ask her you've seen her playing and you'd like to play with her as your playmate. It doesn't matter at all if she refuses. The first contact was made. The next time you see her at the club you are allowed to make a salutation, and she must response to you (if she is a lady). You are not strangers anymore. Now you are someone "she knows from the club".

It is even better if you find out that the lady goes out with her friends to a bar, for example. You may ask your friends (choose the best looking ones) to go there some day. When the two groups find themselves in the bar, you will be the one who knows one of the ladies (the one you like), so you'll have the perfect excuse to get closer to the female group and ask them (in general) if the two groups could be combined. If they agreed, there you've got your first date with the lady.

## What to do, What to say in the first date

The first date is something that is not so structured to be placed in a book. Most of it depends on the lady and the gentlemen. There is not a "plot", or a rigid dialog that has to be said everywhere, and every time. However, there are some rules that a gentleman has to follow when he is in his first date with a lady.

---

1.  By the time this book was written, they are very famous actors and heartbreakers. I don't know when you'll be reading this book, but if you don't know who they are, it would be a sign that this book has become a classic.

- Words like "tits", "breasts" and "asshole" are forbidden in the first contacts. A gentleman does not mention the female's parts of the body that are connected with the sexual intercourse.

- The nastiest words are **ALWAYS** forbidden. (Not only in the first date, but even when the gentleman knows deeply the lady). Example: Gentleman and ladies do not *"fuck"*. Only truck drivers and whores do it. Ladies just make love or have (sexual) relationships. Forget this nasty word that starts with "F". It doesn't have to be a part of your vocabulary. It doesn't matter if everybody uses it. You don't have to do it. If you are an educated man, NEVER say you want to *"fuck"* a lady.

- Some other dirty words that have to be erased permanently from your vocabulary are those ones that allude to the sexual organs, such as "pussy", "cunt", "dick", etc.: Gentleman and Ladies have genitals, or sexual organs. They don't need those descriptive words to refer to them. A gentleman doesn't mention them to a lady.

- A gentleman is not "pride" of his sexual performance and adventures (or at least he doesn't talk about them). He never makes comments that allude to the fact that he is a superlative lover, or that he's had a lot of women, or that he has a *"big"* sexual organ. Truck drivers believe that they excite their women telling them sentences like *"You'll never find someone bigger that me"*, or something similar. This comments are rude and may sound vulgar to a lady.

- Never ask a lady to tell you the number of her ex-boyfriends. If you really want to know about the sexual resume of a lady, wait until she is your official fiancée before asking her. A real gentleman never asks about these things. From the point of view of a gentleman, the lady was a virgin before he met her. (Even if he knows she wasn't). If you are a girl, never horrify your partner telling him how many men you've REALLY had in your life. If you want to talk about it, it is enough (in general) to mention the last one, the first one, and some other in the middle. A gentleman doesn't want to hear that his lady had 25 lovers in the last ten years. It doesn't matter how many lovers the lady has got in her life. The difference between her and a street walker is not the number of men they had, but their respective manners.

IMPORTANT: I want to remember the reader what is has been said in the last two chapters: This is a book of manners, not a book of morality. Here we are discussing the attitudes that a gentleman and a lady should have, from the point of view of education. Many times, manners and moral follow equal rules, but that is not necessarily true at all times. We don't encourage here any "moral" behavior, just educated manners. Example: From the point of view of morality, a girl that enjoys sex and has had many lovers in her life is promiscuous. From our point of view, this classification is irrelevant. The only thing that matters is that this woman should behave as a lady with every one of them. A girl might have had 100 lovers, and she can still be a lady.

# Lessons extracted from Chapter three.

- Ladies do not accept proposals from strangers. Trust is the key for a proper first contact. A gentleman has to find out a way to let her know something about him before he makes a proposal.

- Gentlemen do not "pick up" girls. They do not say nasty or rude words to women in the street.

- Words like "tits", "breasts", "rear", etc. are forbidden. A gentleman does not mention them to a lady when he wants to seduce her.

- The ideal situation is to find someone who knows both the gentleman and the lady and can introduce themselves.

- If this is not possible, you have to find out the things the other person does. Find an activity you can both do together, and a place where it may seem "natural" to ask him/her about it. If he/she refuses, it doesn't matter. The first contact was made in a proper way. The next time you see him/her, you can feel free to say "hello". At this moment you are not strangers anymore, but "someone I know from school", or "classmates". This gives you a better chance to be accepted when you ask her to go out in the future.

- If the other person goes with his/her friends to a bar or club, make a group with your own friends and go there. There you've got an excellent chance to get the first date. As you "know her from school", you can suggest the two groups to join, and VOILA! You've got your date.

# 4

## *T is for Talking.*

## *The importance of communication*

### To communicate or not to communicate: That is the question...

Communication is perhaps one of the most notorious differences between cavern men and gentlemen.

Truck drivers do not communicate with their women. "Real men" don't do it either. The same happens with those men who consider themselves they are very "machos". It seems that many groups of people think that this is not a very important part of the relationships between men & women.

I just ask myself: Why?

Perhaps the most suitable answer is that they don't communicate because they have nothing to communicate. In other words, they don't have anything in their heads.

A lady doesn't want to go out with a rude truck driver, so one of the things she has to value in a gentleman is his intelligence. Street walkers don't care about the intelligence of their lovers. As a matter of fact, a truck driver's girlfriend does not pretend to find erudition in him. It is enough is he is a good lover...

Well, the way we communicate is perhaps the most evident sign of our intellectual skills. In other words, the lack of communication is a mirror where we can see reflected our lack of intelligence.

A gentleman should also be an intelligent person. We have already said that ladies do not prefer rude men, so an educated man has to cultivate the art of the personal communications.

The following tables I and II contains a summary of the basic themes that a gentleman should tell a lady, when they have started to go out together. (and vice versa).

**Table I**
**What every honorable man**
**should (and should not) tell a lady.**

| Theme/Subject | Degree/Amplitude |
|---|---|
| His job or profession | **\*Minimum.** The lady must know what he does to make a living, where he works and the time when he arrives home, but she is not interested in the way he makes deals with the customers, or in the profits of his company in the last quarter. |
| His ex-girlfriends | **\*Minimum.** A honorable man lets his lady feel that she is the first one. He mentions the former girlfriends only if it is strictly necessary. |
| His ex-wife (for men who are divorced) | **\*Absolutely Minimum.** The honorable man just have to tell his lady that he has been married in the past. |

| Theme/Subject | Degree/Amplitude |
|---|---|
| His opinions about his ex-wife | **\*Forbidden**<br>Only if she asks, he can tell her in a summary way what happened ONLY ONCE. If the man thinks his ex-wife is a "bloody witch", it is HIS problem. He must omit to tell his opinion in a loud voice. A gentleman does not involucrate his actual lady with affairs that are concerned with the ex. |
| Sports, football, basketball, his favorite team, the superbowl, and related things | **\*Minimum.**<br>Gentlemen must know that in general ladies DO NOT LIKE men's sports.<br><br>They don't care about the masters tournament. For them, the superbowl is the recipient where the salad must be placed.<br><br>The lady will realize that her man loves baseball in a way or another, he doesn't have to be eloquent about this act. |
| His opinions about Art, literature, music, theater etc. | **\*Yes Indeed!**<br><br>Anyone who presumes to be a gentleman, MUST have an opinion about arts.<br><br>The honorable man doesn't need to be an expert in arts, but he must have an average education.<br><br>A lady expects to find a man who knows something (at least) about art.<br><br>Sometimes it is just enough if he tells her he loves to go to the theatre, for example…<br><br>However, if he is an expert in abstract paintings and modern sculptures, he has a competitive advantage over other men. Ladies are repealed by vulgarity and are attracted by erudition. |

| Theme/Subject | Degree/Amplitude |
|---|---|
| His opinions about politics, religion, racism, political preferences, etc. | **\*It depends**<br><br>If the lady likes politics, or is involved in any political force, then the gentleman must speak about it.<br><br>If the lady does not mention these subjects, the educated man has to avoid any chat related to them, because it means that she is not interested.<br><br>A lady will feel bored if her fiancée talks to her about things she doesn't care about. |
| His opinions about the role of the family in his life, education, children, an ideal place to live, his plans for the future, his projects in life, etc. | **\*Definitively YES!**<br>(If the man is planning to have a long-term relationship)<br><br>If we are in presence of a short-term loving relationship (let's call it an "affair"), it would be more delicate if the man does not mention any of these themes. |
| His positive opinions about the way the lady looks like | **\*Always**<br><br>Gentlemen have to remark things like these:<br><br>\*The lady is wearing a new, sensual dress.<br>\*The lady has got a new look.<br>\*She's gone to the hairdressers, and has her hair professionally combed.<br>\*She's on a diet, so she looks thinner. |
| His negative opinions about the way the lady looks like | **\*Absolutely minimum!!**<br><br>A gentleman DOES NOT criticize his lady.<br>If he thinks the way she wears is not appropriate for a specific event, he might suggest her to find out the way the other women will look like, the kind of dresses they usually wear etc. |

| Theme/Subject | Degree/Amplitude |
|---|---|
| | **\*NEVER!!** |
| | Never say to a lady she is fat, or that she looks old! |
| His negative opinions about the body of the lady | If a lady asks her fiancée if he thinks that she is fat, he must reply something diplomatic, like: "If you are thinking about a diet, I'd join you…we could make it together".<br>A man can tell his lady she needs a diet without being rude… |
| | 99% of women feel uncomfortable with their bodies. Most of them think they are fat, and the rest that they are too thin. The ideal body for a woman is: |
| | • 90 cm–35" (breasts) |
| | • 60 cm–23" (waist) |
| | • 90 cm–35" (hips) |
| | The average woman does not have a body that matches these standards. |
| | Many women that have small breasts dream about a plastic surgery to modify that. |
| | An educated man NEVER asks his lady to enlarge her breasts! It is absolutely vulgar and pejorative to tell a lady to do that!.<br>If SHE feels she wants to do it, the man can support her, but if she doesn't mention it, the educated man can't say a word about this theme. Think about this: |
| | Many women stand their husbands even though they have overweight. If they do it, an educated husband can stand a wife with small breasts. A lady doesn't need to look like a porno star. |

### Table II
### What every lady
### should (and should not) tell a man.

| Theme/Subject | Degree/Amplitude |
|---|---|
| Her job or profession | **Minimum.**<br><br>A lady must avoid to be overwhelming when she talks about her work.<br><br>It is not polite if she stresses her fiancée talking too much about it. She must realize that in general a man is interested in her, not in her profession. |
| Her ex-boyfriends | **\*Just if necessary.**<br><br>A lady must speak as less as possible about her ex-boyfriends. She must NEVER compare his actual fiancée with them.<br><br>Sentences as:<br>—"*Peter used to do it better*",—(where Peter is an ex) are forbidden. |
| Her ex-husband (for women who are divorced) | **\*Do not mention him.**<br><br>The figure of the ex-husband irritates the average man. If the lady still remembers him in any way, she must do it on her own. Certain things doesn't have to be shared with other persons. |
| Her opinions about her ex-husband | **\*Just to talk with her female friends.**<br><br>It is possible that she thinks her ex is a "*miserable pig*".<br><br>However, a lady doesn't have to tell this kind of things to her fiancée. |

| Theme/Subject | Degree/Amplitude |
|---|---|
| Her opinions about art, literature, music, theater etc. | **\*Very carefully!**<br><br>A lady can show that she is an educated person and talk about arts, but she must be very careful when she does it. She just have to mention the subjects. If the man answers and shows interest in them, then she can display her knowledge. However, if the man is evasive, this is a sign that she doesn't have to talk about this things.<br>Remember: A lady can be more erudite than her fiancée, but she must NEVER humiliate him showing this fact. |
| Her opinions about international politics, religion, racism, political preferences, etc | **\*In general: YES**<br><br>An average man will value a lady that is informed about the social reality. |
| Her opinions about the role of the family in her life, education, children, an ideal place to live, her plans for the future, her projects in life, etc. | **\*Very risky in the first dates!**<br><br>A man may feel pressed by the woman. Many men have problems to express their feelings to their girlfriends.<br><br>Sometimes it is hard for them to say simple things as "I love you". It is not very easy for many of them.<br><br>All these questions may be understood by a man as an intent to press him to express his feelings, and he might feel that this attitude is overwhelming.<br><br>A lady has to be very diplomatic with these subjects. |

| Theme/Subject | Degree/Amplitude |
|---|---|
| Her opinions about the way the man looks like | **\*Be careful with this also...**<br><br>If the opinions are favorable, the lady may make a comment about that. However, an average man is not expecting to receive too many considerations of this kind, so he might feel uncomfortable if the woman is too enthusiastic.<br><br>If the opinions are negative, the woman has to be diplomatic. It is not proper to tell a man he is fat, for example. A lady should have to suggest him that perhaps he'd need to make more sports. A lady should NEVER humiliate a man telling him his failures directly. |

# Lessons extracted from Chapter Four.

- Truck drivers do not communicate with their women. Many groups of people think that this is not a very important part of the relationships between men & women.

- An educated man has to cultivate the art of the personal communications.

- A gentleman doesn't have to talk to his lady about:

  - His job or profession

  - His ex-girlfriends

  - His ex-wife (for men who are divorced)

  - His opinions about his ex-wife

  - Sports, football, basketball, his favorite team, the super bowl, etc.

- A gentleman talks to his lady about:

  - The role of the family in his life

  - Education

  - children

  - An ideal place to live

  - His plans for the future

  - His projects in life

  - His positive opinions about the way the lady looks like

- A lady doesn't have to talk to her man about:

  - Her job or profession

  - Her ex-boyfriends (or girl-friends)

  - Her ex-husband (for women who are divorced)

  - Her opinions about her ex-husband

- A lady has to talk to her man about:

  - Arts, music, theater (if he likes these subjects)

  - Her opinions about international politics, religion, racism, political preferences, etc

- A lady has to be very diplomatic and careful when she talks about :

  - Family, education, children, etc. (A man could think she is looking anxiously for a husband. Some of them could find this attitude scaring)

  - Her opinions about the way the man looks like (if this is something negative)

# 5

# *The first date and the first time you do it: What to say, where to avoid it .*

## What to do when the time has come

The first question a gentleman has to ask himself is when has the moment come to have sex. This is a conflictive point in the western culture. We all know that in our culture a lady might be considered as "easy" if she shows too explicitly her sexual desires. An "easy" woman is not seen as a lady, so a gentleman has to suggest he's willing to have sex without being overwhelming to the lady. It requires a bit of diplomacy from him to test her mood in order to ask her about it.

## Is it proper to go to bed in the first date?

Truck drivers and prostitutes do it, so it means that ladies and gentlemen shouldn't. It is not a question of Puritanism; it is more related to education.

There is not a written law that says "A lady doesn't go to bed in the first date". However, it is an excellent time for her to let the man proof that he is indeed a gentleman, and that he doesn't want to "force" the relationship. A man that is too urged to have sex is not a gentleman, and ladies must try to perceive this. They need a man who could be able to respects her internal times.

## What are we suppose to do in the first date?

There is not a single model to express what actions should happen in the first date. However, these steps are the standard behavior expected for the event:

- The gentleman goes to the lady's home: It is more educated this way. However, sometimes she prefers to meet him in a neutral place, such as a restaurant. What it is important here is that the gentleman should ask the lady about her preference.

- The gentleman takes her somewhere: He must try to find a place where she feels comfortable. It can be a restaurant, a theater, a cinema, or a disco. The educated man must choose an appropriate environment for the first date. There is a strategy here: If the gentleman wants to talk to her in the first date, he must suggest a restaurant. If he prefers to speak less (because he feels he doesn't know what to say, or he is too shy), a theatre or a cinema is the best option. The same concept is valid for ladies. She might suggest the gentleman about going to the cinema or to a restaurant. I personally don't like discos as the proper environment for a first date (there are too noisy and in general they are not a very romantic place). However, I don't object if the man thinks it is a good idea to take her there.

- They go back together to her home: Gentlemen NEVER ask their ladies to go back alone to their homes in the first date. In general, ladies don't refuse to return home with them.

- They come home (her home), and they say goodbye: Well…Here's the moment where all the fist date will be summarized. This is most important moment of all. Here is when the manners of the gentleman and the lady appears. In general, three things may happen here:

  a.  The lady liked the date and she indeed wants to go out with him again.

  b.  The date was so-so, but it wasn't cool at all.

  c.  She didn't like it and she doesn't want to go out with him anymore.

## What does she has to do under these circumstances?

In general, ordinary girls DO NOT act properly in these moments.

Ladies must dominate the art of diplomacy in order to let the man know what she feels without being rude or apprehensive. This is an art. If she liked the boy, and she wants to let him know about this, all she has to do is to stare him directly to his eyes, and smile to him. If he moves towards her, she can adopt a position that implies she wants to be kissed. This is the easiest situation. As we've said before, it is more educated if this first date ends at this moment. If she wants to tell him she wants to go out again, she may tell him something like

—*"Fortunately, I don't have to go to (**any place is the same here**), so I'll be free on Wednesday evening…".*

All the gentleman has to do is to coordinate the next date…

If the date wasn't cool enough but the man acted as a gentleman, good manners indicate that the lady should give him a second chance. Many uneducated girls refuse to go out with these boys just because they didn't feel they were in the "limbo" the first time. This is very rude.

In these circumstances (saying goodbye the first time), she doesn't need to show explicitly she wants to be kissed, and she doesn't have to tell him about her future activities, but she should have to let him know her telephone number. If he is interested in her, he will call soon.

A lady always give a second chance to a gentleman. (Remember that he has to act like one. Cavern men don't deserve a second chance, nor a second minute of her time).

What happens if she didn't like him?

## How to tell a man she doesn't want to go out again without being rude:

As we said before, many women do not know what to do in these circumstances, so they adopt rude and uneducated behaviors. A lady must dominate the art of saying "NO" to a man without hurting his feelings.

If he wants to kiss her, she must be flexible enough to refuse him with elegance. First of all, she has to prepare the environment. It means that she has to establish physical distance between them diplomatically. If he wants to be closer to her, she has to accelerate or slow down the way she walks just to be in a position where he can not touch her.

This is a first warning for a gentleman. If the girl you are dating doesn't get close to you, it means that she is not attracted to you enough.

When they are saying goodbye to each other, the lady must anticipate the intention of the man to kiss her and say goodbye before he attempts to do that. For example, she could say with a gentle voice

—*"Thank you to have asked me to go out with you…Goodbye…"*, *or something similar.*

Note that a lady is always polite, so she thanks the man even if she didn't like him. This way the man won't feel humiliated. If he phones her again, she has to say something like

—*"I'm really sorry but I'm actually not prepared to start a new relationship with a man"*,—or something similar.

It is very important that the words she uses could be as soft as she can. In other words, a lady doesn't need to lie in order to refuse a man, but she can say the facts in such a way that his self esteem could remain intact.

## Things a girl doesn't have to say when she wants to refuse a man:

As we said before, many uneducated women do not know what to say when they want to refuse a man, so they behave in a rude and cruel way. These are some sentences that should be avoided by ladies. Let's keep them for the use of street walkers.

Examples:

—*Don't phone me, I'll phone you*—When a woman says that, you have to take for granted the fact that she won't phone him again. If a woman says so, she is being irreverent with the man. She is lying, and she is also insulting him. Any intelligent man will recognize this lie, and he will feel humiliated, because he will realize that the girl thinks he is so stupid he will believe in such a lie.

—*I'm dating with another man*—This is a very effective sentence to let him know she doesn't want him to phone again, but has two effects:

    a.    The man feels she is a street walker that goes out with two men at the same time

b.   He also feels that she could have warned him before he asked her to go out, so he feels "used"

—*I don't want you to call again*—It is very effective but too direct and rude. A lady has to dominate the arts of diplomacy.

—*I'm married*—Effective too, but it denotes she is an unfaithful woman, who uses other people to satisfy her desires. A lady should not say that.

—*Fuck you, asshole!*—Let it for the use of prostitutes. Do not copy the way they speak

## Where to do it. Where to avoid it

Well…suppose you have passed the first date. As a matter of fact, you have been going out with the other person for some time and now you are ready to have an intercourse. The question is: Where do you have to do it?

Let's think a bit about it:

The ideal utopist place could be a very romantic desert island, or a desert beach, under the light of the moon…Of course, you have to be on holidays in a tropical location to do it this way.

More realistic alternatives: If the gentleman is old enough, he should have a flat, or a house. This could be the ideal place. Perhaps the lady has got a flat too. In this case it would also be a perfect place. Many ladies feel more comfortable at their own houses, so it is a very good strategy for men to be there when they want to start having intercourse. These are the best places of them all to do it for the first time. What we'd have to talk a bit now is what happens when it is not possible to do that.

The second possible best site is a friend's house. If the gentleman doesn't have his own house, he might ask a single friend to lend him his house for some hours. This could be acceptable too.

A motel is a possible place, but it is not very romantic…A gentleman should only use this alternative if none of the others are feasible. A lady doesn't want to be taken to a motel if there is another alternative available.

The last option we have to talk about is the American way: The back seat of a car, parked in a quiet place:
I personally consider it is not romantic at all. Teenagers do it all the time, but they are not gentlemen, they are grown up kids. I know that many couples have been made this way, and I know that many of us have done it in a car sometimes, but this is a book about manners, and I really think that a car shouldn't have to be the first option to take a lady to do it.

In summary: A gentleman should have to care about the place where he will take the lady to do it for the first time. It is not polite to try to do it everywhere. Truck drivers do it in their dirty vehicles. A gentleman has to be more careful about it.

# Lessons extracted from
# Chapter Five.

- There is not a written law that says "A lady doesn't go to bed in the first date". However, it is an excellent time for her to let the man proof that he is indeed a gentleman, and that he doesn't want to "force" the relationship.

- Ladies must dominate the art of diplomacy in order to let the man know what she feels without being rude or apprehensive. In general, ordinary girls do not act properly in these moments.

- A gentleman must know that if the girl doesn't get close to him, it means that she is not attracted enough by his presence.

- There are some things a girl doesn't have to say when she wants to refuse a man, as—*"Don't phone me, I'll phone you"*—. A lady refuses a man in a polite way, but she doesn't have to lie to do it.

- A gentleman cares about the place where he will take the lady to do it for the first time. It is not polite to try to do it everywhere.

# 6

# *Preparing the scene: The proper environment*

○ ○ ○ ○ ○ ○ ○ ○ ○ ○ ○ ○ ○ ○ ○ ○ ○ ○ ○ ○ ○ ○ ○ ○ ○ ○ ○ ○ ○ ○ ○
*Power is the way we call our skills to change our environment. However, to do it, we first have to change ourselves. Perseverance is power. Self trust is power.*

## What to do to make things work as expected

We've said in the previous chapter that the best sites to do it were the idyllic desert island, or the gentleman's house, at least. Well, let's suppose now that the educated man is preparing his home to receive the lady. We will talk about it now.

A gentleman takes care about the environment the lady will see, and tries to make it suitable for her presence. Truck drivers just do it in the dirty seats of their trucks. A gentleman has to be more delicate about these themes.

Always remember that a lady has to find the place comfortable. A lady values the fact that her man has paid attention to all details. The first thing he has to do is to have his flat clean. The living room must be clean, the bed must be made, with clean sheets. The bathroom must be clean. A lady may desire to have a bath after the act, so the bathroom must be in conditions to let her do it. There must be clean towels in it. **A gentleman has to go to the laundry before asking a girl to go to his home.** The gentleman should reserve a new, clean towel for the exclusive use of the lady in the bathroom. When they know each other better they can share the towels, but the first times it is better to use separate ones. It is a good attitude to place a new, unused soap in the bathroom.

It is absolutely improper to take a lady to a place where the bathroom is dirty, for example. A lady may refuse to do it in a place where she doesn't feel comfortable.

If the flat has some rancid odor, some deodorant must be flushed in the air. It is not a bad idea to buy some roses and to put them in the living room. This will cause a good impression to her.

In the fridge there must be either wine or champagne, to offer her something to drink. It is very appropriate to give her cold white wine, for example. Mineral water is also needed. **Many women do not drink alcohol, so they will ask for a glass of water. When a lady asks for it, it means "Eau Perrier", not an ordinary glass of water.** A gentleman has to have at least one bottle in the fridge reserved for the lady.

The use of aromatic candles is also a detail that a lady values. Actually there are lots of aromatic flavors that can be obtained without too much effort. Fruits, and fresh country herbs (as lavender) are the coolest flavors for an aromatic candle. A big one or two small ones are enough for a standard living room.

## Music and sounds

We all have in mind the typical scene: The lady goes to the gentleman's apartment, and he offers her a drink and then some music bewitches the air…

Well, there are some things to say about music and romance…

First of all, the gentleman doesn't have to show the woman his electronic devices. If he has a big CD player or the last model of quadraphonic baffles, that is not a point to remark to the lady. He just have to use them as naturally as possible. If she likes audio and technology, she'll let the man know about it. If the lady doesn't say anything it means she doesn't care about those "toys".

It is better if the gentleman just selects a sweet and romantic melody. If it is a classic song, it is better. Forget everything related with rap, funk, etc. They are not appropriate for these moments. If a gentleman doesn't know what to select, it is better to play nothing. If the lady is sophisticated indeed, classic music is a good choice. I personally prefer Chopin as a background music for these circumstances. (But this is just my personal taste). It is extremely romantic, and prepares the mood of the lady in a positive way. At the same time the lady perceives that she is in front of an educated gentleman.

If the lady says she prefers the last hit she heard on the radio yesterday, well…she is demonstrating that she was not so well educated…

What is important to emphasize here is that music talks about the soul of the gentleman (or the lady). Educated persons have a wide musical culture. This means that at least they have a certain knowledge of classic music and jazz. Some of them also like some kind of ethnic music, just like Celtic folk music or the rhythms from the Andes.

The important thing to notice here is that if all you know about music are some lyrics emanated from some bluegrass songs, you should enlarge your musical knowledge a bit before dating a gentleman (or a lady).

# Lessons extracted from
# Chapter Six.

- A gentleman takes care about the environment the lady will see, and tries to make it suitable for her presence.

- It is absolutely improper to take a lady to a place where the bathroom is dirty, for example. A gentleman has to go to the laundry before asking a girl to go to his home.

- When a lady asks for a glass of water, it means she wants "Eau Perrier". Ordinary water is just to clean the dishes.

- The use of aromatic candles is also a detail that a lady values.

- A gentleman doesn't have to show a lady his electronic video devices. If she likes audio and technology, she'll let the man know about it.

- Music talks about the soul of the gentleman (or the lady). Educated people have a wide musical culture.

# 7

## *An educated gentleman is not in love with his car*

o o o o o o o o o o o o o o o o o o o o o o o o o o o o o o o o o o

*Ordinary men have to be trained. They have to understand, for example, that their cars are not an extension of their sexual organs.*

## Thou shall not desire thy neighbor's car

In general, educated ladies consider that a man who talks too much about his car is a fool. (Remember that a lady doesn't say things like "asshole"). Always remember that a lady doesn't value a man who is "in love with his car". They think he is a "chauvinist macho", and those words are absolutely inappropriate for a gentleman.

If you are a man, always remember this:

- Your car is a machine that you have to use to drive your lady to the restaurant (or to drive her home). As a matter of fact, if you don't think so, don't even mention it to her.

- Women don't care about the engine of your car, or how many layers of painting has it got. Talk about these facts with your mechanic, not with a lady.

The following table gives us some examples about attitudes that are inadequate for a gentleman:

### Men & their cars:
### What to do—What to avoid

| IF | Expected behavior from a Gentleman : |
|---|---|
| *A lady asks her boy-friend to teach her how to drive (using his car for practicing, of course) | *It is not a catastrophe (for a gentleman, of course). He doesn't have to feel that his life has been ruined suddenly. If he is terrified about the fact that she could cause a tiny scratch to his beloved car, then he might suggest, (in his best lovingly voice), that he is not a professional driving instructor, and she deserves the best, so a professional driving course could be the best option. If this is the case, the gentleman has to find out about courses, places and fees. When we are talking about something related with mechanics (and cars indeed are!), ladies want solutions, not problems. An educated man has to give her solutions: She wants to hear something like: <br><br>—*Darling, I've arranged everything. Tomorrow at 6 pm you've got your first class. Don't worry, I'll drive you there. Just be ready at 5.30"*— |
| *The lady wants him to take her to the theatre (or the opera, or something similar) | *The car has to be washed and cleaned. The gentleman has to wash the car (or take it to the car washing machine) before the event. |
| *The lady smokes in the car. | *If some of the ashes drop outside the ashtray, it is not the end of the world. A gentleman does NOT recriminate his lady if she throws ashes in the car's carpet. By the way, a lady always uses the car's ashtray (if she smokes). |

| *IF* | *Expected behavior from a Gentleman :* |
|---|---|
| *The lady closes the car's door with energy | *The educated man doesn't have to show his anger to her. If the noise of the door knocking against the car was like a bullet directed to the deepest part of his hart, he doesn't have to mention it. He doesn't have to check the door in front of the lady to see if it is damaged. If he indeed wants to say something, he just have to say:<br><br>—*"Fortunately, darling, this car was made in such a way that the doors close with very little energy. You don't need to use your impulse to close it. Isn't it marvelous?..."* |
| *A lady feels sick in the car. (A lady doesn't get drunk because she always drinks with moderation, so we must suppose that this problem is something related with her stomach, or perhaps she is pregnant) | *A gentleman just have to drive her home at normal speed. He doesn't have to rush, nor enter into a state of panic thinking that maybe she could eventually vomit in his beloved car. If this event happens, all he has to say is something like: —*"It doesn't matter at all, dear; the only important thing here is your health"*<br><br>In other words: A gentleman NEVER complains if a lady accidentally makes any damage to the car or gets it dirty. |
| *A lady forgets a personal object in the car, or she lets it there on purpose. | *A lady can let in the car whatever she wants. A gentleman doesn't have to take out of it the object, unless she asks for it. If he finds there her glasses, for example, he has to leave them there until she requests for them. It is not improper to remind her that her glasses are at the car, but if the gentleman uses to take off all of her things, the lady will start to think that her presence is not welcomed at his car. Always remember that the lady has to feel comfortable everywhere when she is with the man. This implies that she must also feel comfortable at the car. |

# Lessons extracted from
# Chapter Seven.

- Educated ladies consider that a man who talks too much about his car is a fool.

- Women don't care about engines, tires, or layers of painting. If you are a man, talk about these things with your mechanic.

- If she asks him to teach her how to drive (using his beloved car), this is not a catastrophe.

- The car has to be washed and cleaned. A man does not have to ask his girl-friend to go out with a dirty car.

- If the lady is smoking in the car and some ashes drop outside the ashtray, it is not a good excuse to start a quarrel.

- If she closes the car's door with energy, he doesn't have to get angry. If this drives him crazy, it is just his problem, not hers.

# PART III
## All roads drive to sex

# 8

## *The way you wear: Sexual Garments*

○ ○ ○ ○ ○ ○ ○ ○ ○ ○ ○ ○ ○ ○ ○ ○ ○ ○ ○ ○ ○ ○ ○ ○ ○ ○ ○ ○ ○ ○ ○ ○ ○

*Not everyone are lucky enough to get things for free. In general, we have to fight for them. Freedom is not a gift. It has never been. It is merely the treasure we've got when we combat against our fears. Freedom must be conquered. There is no option, you can be a free man or a slave. It is up to you.*

## Elegance is the name of the game

*Ladies and gentlemen must be elegant. Let vulgarity for street walkers and truck drivers.*

It is not possible to give specific advices about the way a lady and a gentleman must wear, but there are indeed some general premises that have to be commented here:

This is both for men and women:

It doesn't matter what you wear, but how personal and elegant is the way you do it.

A lady must have charm. It is a prerogative for her. A gentleman must be personal in the way he looks like.

Ordinary people do not know the difference between being personal and being elegant. In general, women believe that being on fashion is a way of being elegant.

Always remember this: There is nothing wrong if you use one or two things that are on fashion. However, those people who are always worried about it are not elegant people, they are just brainless automats.

A gentleman doesn't have a very good opinion about a woman who is always "on fashion". He thinks she is stupid.

---

Elegance is frequently related to classicism. Elegant people wear in a classic way.

---

However, the really trend setters are the ones that can combine successfully the concepts "classic"+"personal".

It doesn't matter what you wear, but if you can use your garments in such a way that the people identifies them with you, you will have your "style". Both ladies and gentleman love the ones who have style. People who wear with style have charm.

One amazing point: You don't have to be formal to be elegant!. You can be wearing sport garments and still be charming. As a matter of fact, your personal style may be related to the fact that you wear informal clothes...

For example, my personal style is related with comfort. I always try to use comfortable clothes, so I try to wear comfortable trousers and wide jackets. This is my style. Other people play with the colors. For example, they play with the blue tones, so they use their garments in such a way that everything they use is related with blue.

It is always useful to remember that ladies assimilate the dark colors with masculinity, while soft and creamy pastel colors are related to girls.

So, dark blues, marine blues, and dark grays are colors for gentlemen.

Light blues, pinks, grays and yellows are ideal for the ladies.

Last week I saw a very elegant lady. She wasn't wearing something very sophisticated at all. She only had some white trousers and a crochet sweater in white and light pink tones. Very feminine.

---

To dress like a lady is not a question of money: It is a matter of good taste.

---

## Is lingerie a matter of street walkers?: Being a lady even if you are only using underwear

Another point we have to remark is the elegance of men & women when they take out their clothes.

You have to be elegant even when you are in underwear.

The question is now: What kind of clothes do we need to wear in these moments?

The following table instructs us about which clothes we should wear and which ones we should avoid in these circumstances.

Underwear: What to wear—What to avoid

| Facts | An educated person must |
|---|---|
| **MEN** | |
| *What to wear | *Boxers, in general. Monochromatic (only one color) if possible |
| | *Prefer standard models |
| | *White, blue, gray and black are good tones |

| Facts | An educated person must |
|---|---|
| *What to avoid to wear | *Do not use bikini-size men's underwear if you are fat. (In some countries they are called **slips**, so we'll use this name for them). Slips are just for men who have a good body. A fat man in slip looks like a gorilla in a bath suit.<br><br>*Slips, (in particular). NEVER use those "erotic" slips that have the colors and patterns of a tiger, a cheetah, or any other animal. The person who uses them looks like an animal himself (or should I say itself?).<br><br>*Leather underwear/Black leather boxers: If you know your lady is a disciple of the *Marquis de Sade* and she loves to have a session of love of these characteristics, perhaps you could use leather clothes. In any other case it is not recommended to use them. |
| **WOMEN** | |
| *What to wear | *Sexual liberation has nothing to do with elegance. Ladies should use brassiere when they go out with a gentleman. To have your breasts moving from right to left when you are walking is not the expected behavior of a lady.<br><br>*In general the bra and the panties should be of the same color. In some particular cases, it is allowed to break this rule, but they are just that: Exceptions. (Ex: if the lady is wearing some white trousers and a dark blouse, she could use a dark bra, and a white panty.<br><br>*Lingerie*bodies* are recommended for women who have a bit of overweigh. If you don't have a perfect body, it is better to make an insinuation than to show directly what you've got.<br><br>*In general, most men are excited if the lady uses lingerie. (they have a lot of synthetic components). However, many women say they prefer cotton underwear, because they are fresh and comfortable, so here ladies have got a moment of decision: If they want to excite their men, they should use lingerie. If they want to be fresh, they should use cotton as a personal style. |

| Facts | An educated person must |
|---|---|
| *What to avoid | *Vivid colors, such as bright yellow. Female's underwear doesn't have to look like a Hawaiian bath suit. |
| | *Panties and bikinis that have the colors and patterns of a tiger, a panther, or some other animal. This is what it is expected to see in prostitutes. A lady doesn't have to look like a hooker. |
| | *Panties that have the colors of a football club. There are indeed some men that are fanatic of a football (or soccer, or baseball) team. They encourage their women to buy these kind of things. Some women buy them just to turn their men on. This perhaps could be understandable for a teenager cheerleader that goes out with the team's captain, but it is not proper for a lady. |
| | Remember this: A gentleman doesn't "turn on" with these clothes. He won't even mention it to her fiancée. A lady doesn't "turn him on" showing him she uses the colors of his team. This is vulgar, and from our point of view, obscenity is related with vulgarity, so we can say it is obscene. |
| | *Black leather bras or panties: Only allowed if he is a fan of the *Marquis de Sade*, and you love this fact. If you use them, don't say anything if he tries to have violent sex with you… |
| *Warnings for women | *Red underwear: Some men are excited by red lingerie, but some others think it is for prostitutes. Before using this color, you have to know deeply the man you are going out with. |

# Lessons extracted from
# Chapter Eight.

- Ladies and gentlemen must be elegant. Let vulgarity for street walkers and truck drivers.

- It doesn't matter what you wear, but how personal and elegant the way you do it is.

- Ordinary people do not know the difference between being personal and being elegant. In general, women believe that being on fashion, is a way of being elegant.

- Elegance is frequently related to classicism. Elegant people wear in a classic way.

- Women assimilate the dark colors with masculinity, while soft and creamy pastel colors are related to girls.

- To dress like a lady is not a question of money: It is a matter of good taste.

# 9

## *Erotism vs. obscenity*

*Drink some nectar, and then kiss me, because I'd love to feel the sweetest possible feeling of the world.*

## Erotic or Obscene?

Our western culture has been obsessed with these two words since the beginning of times. As a matter of fact, they both refer to the same acts. However, they reflect the prejudices of the people who mentions them. This is not a book about erotic behavior itself, but we must explain a bit these terminology in order to talk about the proper manners that a man and a woman must have in bed.

## What is erotic? What is obscene?

As it was said in the previous paragraph, they both refer to the same acts, but they are used to remark the positive and negative side of the same concept.

We use the word "erotic" to define the good and positive aspects of sexuality, not only the act itself, but also the environment and the circumstances that end with the union of a man and a woman in an intercourse. So, we have to notice that the erotic behavior is wider than the sexual act itself.

However, there is a dark side of erotism, that reflects all the improper behavior in this area. To refer to it, we use the word "obscene" or "pornographic". This dualism between erotism and obscenity is typical of our culture. In many traditional societies, sex is not seen as something "good" or "bad" in terms of the way you behave.

Some years ago, I have read the works of the anthropologist Margaret Mead in Samoa islands. That ancient culture was extremely permissive from the sexual point of view. One of the things that we have to remark here from them, is that the meaning of the word "obscene" was something difficult for them to understand. How do you explain what you mean by "obscene" to a culture that does not consider that the sexual behavior has a dark side? It is impossible.

In other words: The inclusion of this chapter in the book is a consequence that derives from the fact that our repressive culture considers that many aspects of sexuality are inadequate and must be punished.

This is a manners book, not a morality tractate, so we'll use here the word "erotic" to show all the behaviors that a gentleman and a lady should have, and "obscene" to all the ones that should be avoided by them. As we said before in the book, a lady has to avoid vulgarity, so we'll use here the word obscene as a synonym of the word *"vulgar"*. This means that for us an obscene behavior is a vulgar one. When we are vulgar, we are obscene.

With these concepts in mind, we are able now to start talking about the proper erotic manners that a gentleman and a lady should have.

As we said before, **vulgarity is the key word that helps us to distinguish between erotism and pornography.**

We could then start this point of the book saying that:

---

*The gentleman and the lady must seek for erotism and must avoid obscenity, when they are intimating.*

---

# Anatomy of vulgarity

The point to discuss now is then: Which attitudes are vulgar? What should I do when I am in bed with my boyfriend/girlfriend? Which things should I refuse to do, even if he/she asks me?

In general, we have to say that truck drivers and prostitutes are vulgar, so we can conclude they are obscene too. Remember that for us vulgarity and obscenity are the same. Anyway, the main point is not what they do, but the way they do it. As we said before, gentlemen have sexual relationships, while truck drivers do that word that starts with "F". The difference between these concepts is the way they do it, not what they are doing...

The following table shows us some usual sexual attitudes and makes a comment about the degree of vulgarity they contain.

### Sexual attitudes & degree of vulgarity

| Attitude | Comments |
|---|---|
| **\*Casual Sex** | |
| Example: | *It is vulgar. |
| **To go to a singles bar, to meet someone and to go to bed after some drinks. | Gentlemen and ladies prefer to have relations with their boyfriends/girlfriends instead of casual sex. To meet someone just to have sex is not elegant at all. |
| **To meet someone at a party and to go to bed. (In general, they don't see each other again in the future) | |
| **\*Mistresses and Lovers**  Example:  Married gentlemen or ladies who have lovers | *Absolutely vulgar and obscene. As it was said before many times, this is not a morality book, so we don't care about if this is moral or not. This is not the point. The fact here is that a gentleman is an educated person indeed!  If you lie to your husband (or wife) to have an affair with your lover, it denotes you are a rude person, a liar. In other words, you are not a gentleman (or a lady). Always remember that the most appreciate possession that a gentleman's got is his word.  If a gentleman doesn't love his wife anymore, he talks to her about it. If she asks for a divorce, he assumes the consequences as a man. You can lose your love towards the other person, but you NEVER have to lose your manners. |

| Attitude | Comments |
|---|---|
| *Oral Sex | *Oral sex itself is not vulgar nor "dirty". Remember that we are not talking here about morality, but manners. |
| | It is not improper to tell your boyfriend/girlfriend you like it. However, there are some rules that should be followed in order to have a good relationship with the other person: |
| | You should ask the other about it. However, in this particular case, you can insinuate the other you are going to do it and expect the reaction. If he/she keeps quiet and says nothing, it is a good sign that he/she will accept it. It is a good attitude to do it first to the other person before you ask him/her to do it to you. |
| | There are some men that ask their ladies for oral sex, but they don't want to do it in response. This is not a proper manner. The proper behavior is: If you like it, you also have to do it to the other person. |
| | Warnings: It is absolutely vulgar and dirty to do it with a person that "has worked all day", (just to say it in a diplomatic way). If your fiancée needs a bath, it is not improper to ask him to go to the shower before you do it. |
| | You can say things like: |
| | —I love to do it with when you have just had a bath— |
| | or something similar, to let the other person know your desires. |
| | Gentlemen and ladies must be clean in order to initiate an intercourse. If they feel they are dirty and the other one pretends to have sexual relationships, they have to alert the other that they haven't taken a bath yet. |

| Attitude | Comments |
|---|---|
| *Anal Sex | *In general this is something that men ask their women about, but it is also something that many women don't want to do. |
| | Anal sex is not vulgar if it is consented. It is not an improper manner if a gentleman asks his girlfriend to do it. |
| | However, many women say it "hurts", so they don't want to do it. A gentleman has to have consideration towards his lady. It is improper to try to force her to do it. A gentleman does not press his lady to do things that hurt. |
| | He can instigate her, but he can't force her to do it. |
| | A gentleman lubricates the area with oils or creams before doing it. If the lady has accepted to have sex using her back, he must be careful enough to spread one of these substances in her body before he attempts to penetrate her. |
| | If he doesn't have any of these substances at home, he must postpone the act for a better moment. Anal sex must not be a torture session for women. He must try to lubricate her as much as possible to prevent friction and pain in the anus area. |

| Attitude | Comments |
|---|---|
| **\*Roll Playing** | |
| Example:<br><br>—*"Let's suppose I am Romeo and you are Juliet"*— | \*Erudite and sophisticated form of romance.<br><br>If you have an actor within, roll playing can be a funny thing to do. It depends on the good taste of the gentleman, to choose an appropriate character to play with the lady.<br><br>Classic themes like "Romeo and Juliet" or "The princess and the knight" can be very provocative and spicy.<br><br>Recommended activity to do when you want to take distance from mediocrity. |
| **\*Use of erotic lingerie** | \*We have make comments about it in the previous chapter. |
| **\*To go to "Motels"**<br>and other public places where you can have an intercourse. | \*In general ladies and gentlemen prefer to do it at home.If some circumstance happens that makes it impossible, then a gentleman has to find an adequate place to do it.<br><br>Cheap motels are vulgar. It is obscene to take a lady there. Only high quality places are acceptable to go with your boyfriend/girlfriend.<br><br>It is proper to refuse to go to a cheap motel if your boyfriend/girlfriend wants to take you there. |
| **\*Use of sexual "toys" and complements** | \*Some women could consider them vulgar. Some men could consider a lady vulgar if she asks them to use one of these devices. To suggest the use of one of these things is not recommended until they both know each other very well. |
| **\*Use of creams, oils and lotions**. | \*Is a good attitude to give him/her a massage with a flavored oil or essence. Recommended attitude. |

| Attitude | Comments |
|---|---|
| **\*Private Nudity:**<br><br>Examples:<br><br>\*\*Exhibition of the naked body to your fiancée.<br><br>\*\*Sleeping in the nude | \*It is not vulgar to do it, in first instance, but the feelings of the other person must be respected. A gentleman may insinuate a lady that he'd like to see her in the nude after the act has finished, but he can't press her to do it. Many women put on again their panties and some other clothes after sex because they are cold. A gentleman has to be considerate in this field. |
| **\*Public nudity and Exhibitionism:**<br><br>Examples:<br><br>Asking your fiancée to do it in a public place, even if there is no one left. (Doing it in the elevator, in a public bathroom, in a taxi, bus, train or airplane, etc.) | \*Many people are excited about the idea of doing it in a place where some other people could discover them (in theory).<br><br>However, not everyone love to do things this way. A gentleman has to be very careful about this things.<br><br>It is not recommended to try to do it before asking the other about the intentions. It is absolutely vulgar to try to force the other person to do it if she/he doesn't want. |
| **\*Moderate sexual fantasies**<br><br>Example:<br><br>\*\*To spread cream in the other's lips and then kiss him/her<br><br>\*\*To ask the other to tie you to the bedroom in the moment of the act<br><br>\*\*To ask the other to do it in a non public place as the brother's house etc. | \*There are not vulgar if the act is mutually consented. In these cases, you have to ask the other person his/her opinion about them before any attempt to do anything.<br><br>If your fiancée requests you to do some of these things, it is not improper to accept. A gentleman or a lady should have to try to satisfy the other's needs if they are not too extreme. |

| Attitude | Comments |
|---|---|
| **\*Extreme sexual fantasies** | |
| Examples: | \*In general they are vulgar and obscene, not from the point of view of morality, but from the point of view of education. |
| To have fantasies about: | |
| Sadism, masochism, zoophile's acts, "golden rains", "dark rains", "fist fucking" etc. | If you'd love to do some of these things, do not tell your fiancée about them until you know each other deeply. It is not improper to deny to do any of them. If your fiancée asks you about your opinion, you may just say you don't like these practices. |
| | It is absolutely improper to try to force or to press the other person to do any of these things when you are in bed. |

# Lessons extracted from
# Chapter Nine

- An obscene behavior is a vulgar attitude. When we are vulgar, we are obscene.

- Vulgarity is the key word that helps us to distinguish between erotism and pornography.

- Attitudes that are vulgar:

  - Casual Sex (A gentleman has girlfriends, he does not go to "singles bars").

  - To have Mistresses and Lovers (If you are married, of course; a gentleman does not have two women at the same time).

  - To go to cheap "Motels" to do it.

  - Extreme sexual fantasies as Sadism, masochism, zoophile's acts, "golden rains", "fist fuckings" etc.

# 10

## *In the nude: Taking our clothes off*

o o o o o o o o o o o o o o o o o o o o o o o o o o o o o o o o

*"Drink to me...*
*Drink to my health...*
*You know I can't drink anymore...*

—*(Picasso's last words)"*

## She said YES!...What do I have to do now

Well...finally after ten chapters of the book, we have arrived to the moment where the gentleman goes to bed with the lady.

What does he have to do? How does she have to behave?. We are not talking here about sexual techniques...Let's suppose that they already know about that...Here we'll focus on the manners that they should have when they are intimating.

In the last chapter we have talked about what we consider obscene behavior. It gives us indeed a guide about what we should do and what we should avoid to do.

Once you have an idea about what things are recommended to do and what is considered obscene, we've got to concentrate in the way we do it, in the details. In many occasions, they make the difference between a gentleman and a truck driver. Let's see some specific attitudes in order to make some comments about them:

## Illumination of the room:

The ideal is to have a room with a minimum illumination. The light of a candle is preferred.

It is a bit morbid if the room is completely dark, and too much illumination is not romantic.

## Taking the clothes off:

Some ladies prefer to be undressed by the gentleman. Some others don't. Once they have entered into the bedroom, he must slowly attempt to undress her. If she keeps quiet, it is a sign that means that she wants to be undressed by the gentleman. If she starts to undress herself, the man has to let her do it.

Sometimes the zippers and the buttons of the ladies' clothes are not so easy to be unbuttoned. (Some men consider than bras are a bit difficult to take off, for example). If the lady perceives that the man has a difficulty while he is trying to do it, she must tell him to stop, and she must undress herself. Sometimes men are too excited and they can't concentrate in what they are doing. It is very embarrassing for a man if he can't take off the clothes of a lady properly, so she must be considerate with him. A lady can undress the man too, but it is better if the first times she lets them do it.

## The best gentlemen always use a condom:

A gentleman has to take care of his lady. This means that he doesn't feel comfortable if he could cause her any kind of damage or if he could hurt her. That's why he uses a condom when he is having sexual relationships. Many men refuse to use a condom. I have heard many excuses in my life. Some of them are:

- I don't "feel" well when I use them
- I want to feel her body
- I feel as if "it" were a prisoner
- I don't like torture chambers (referring to the condom)
- People of my age don't use them

- None of my friends use them
- Real men don't need to use them

All of these excuses only hide the fact that the man is a selfish person who only wants to have a good moment without taking care of the consequences of his acts.

## Why do men have to use condoms?

First of all, there's always the problem of viruses that are transmitted using the sexual via. Syphilis, gonorrhea and AIDS are the most common ones.

When a man and a woman know each other deeply, one of them can ask the other if he/she has one of these problems. If they both say they don't, they can avoid the condom. In the XXI century is not a bad manner to ask the other person if he/she has AIDS (for example).

However, you have to be diplomatic when you ask it. A direct, but sincere chat is useful to clear all these aspects of the relationship. Some people ask for some proofs like a medical certificate. If you don't trust in your boyfriend's word, is a sign you are sleeping with the wrong person.

The second problem is pregnancy. If a man feels comfortable, he may ask his lady about if she uses another contraceptive method, but in general, these kind of confidences requires a good communication with the other person, so the first times is always recommended to use the condom. If a lady is taking the pill, for example, she has to tell this fact to the man, in order to let him know about it.

In other words: A gentleman has to use a condom unless he has talked frankly with the lady and they both know they are not infected by a virus and she is using another contraceptive device.

---

*A man who has relationships with a woman without using a condom (and without knowing if she is using an alternative method) is not a gentleman, but a selfish person. A woman that consents to go to bed with a man that doesn't want to use a condom is not a lady, but a fool.*

---

# Petting and necking:

A gentleman does not have to precipitate what it is inevitable. If a lady has gone to the bedroom with him, and she is naked, it means she wants to do it with him (obviously). However, there is no reason why he has to rush to finish the act. A gentleman takes things easy. A truck driver wants to do it as fast as he can.

A vivid foreplay is advisable. A gentleman does not go "directly to the point". There is not point where to go.

Before the act itself it is advisable to be sure your mouth has a proper breath. If you have been drinking or smoking, you should wash your teeth or eat an eucalyptus candy. A lady doesn't want to realize that her man smells to vodka, and a man doesn't want to know that his lady smokes French cigarettes flavored with black tobacco.

Many people believe that the act itself is just the penetration, so they try to do it as soon as possible.

This is a sign of an act made by truck drivers. A gentleman knows that a lady needs some time before she is excited enough to perform the act, so he kisses her slowly for some time before he tries to do something else.

---

*Foreplay is something unknown for truck drivers and a standard procedure for gentlemen.*

---

# The sounds of love:

—*"You don't hear what I say!"*—

Many women say this sentence to their men when they are quarreling. As a matter of fact, this is also valid in bed. Educated men and women should talk in bed and tell each other their preferences. They should both tell the other what they need and what they like. A lady should drive the gentleman to let him know if he's doing the things alright or not. Words like "more", "deeply", "go on" or "stop" are proper to tell him what he has to do. He can use the same words too. Truck drivers don't speak in bed; they are very busy doing it to hear what she says. At least, they offend their ladies saying nasty words.

## Forbidden words to say to a woman:

A gentleman has to be careful about the kind of things he says in bed to a lady. Dirty words are not appropriate in these circumstances. Some lower-class women may like to be called in a rude way, but in general, ladies do not like to be named this way. Words like "bitch" or similar are not recommended as a way to excite a lady in bed.

# Lessons extracted from
# Chapter Ten

- Illumination of the room: The light of a candle is preferred.

- The best gentlemen always use a condom. A man who has relationships with a woman without using a condom (and without knowing if she is using an alternative method) is not a gentleman, but a selfish person.

- A woman that consents to go to bed with a man that doesn't want to use a condom is not a lady, but a fool.

- A vivid foreplay is advisable. A gentleman does not go "directly to the point". There is not point where to go. Foreplay is something unknown for truck drivers and a standard procedure for gentlemen.

- Educated men and women should talk in bed and tell each other their preferences

# *Epilogue*

The gentleman seduced the lady and they lived the rest of their lives enjoying the pleasure of romance...

Truck drivers and street walkers are still out there...They are still rude and continue to show us their innate lack of erudition.

Now, the question is:

*Which way do you want to live your own life:*
*As a lady or with the manners of a prostitute?*

*Who are you: The gentleman or the truck driver?*
*The educated man or the cavern man?*

The answer is up to you...

# Afterword

o o o o o o o o o o o o o o o o o o o o o o o o o o o o o o o o o o o

*Love looks not with the eyes but with the mind...*

—*William Shakespeare*[1]

The general idea beyond Shakespeare's concept is that love doesn't follow the path of the obvious things. I agree. Love is a feeling that emerges after a vast number of details have happen. As it was said in this book, details are the difference between a gentleman and a beggar. These events are the ones that are recognized by the mind and generate the feeling of what we have called in our culture "love". This book was indeed a work of details. It showed you a vivid collection of them. We use to call them "manners", and "education".

In these chapters I have tried to convince you, reader, that there is another point of view, another way to live life.

I hope I could have been able to persuade you that living as a gentleman (or as a lady) is something worth, and that manners are facts that help us to live deeply our lives.

---

1. I always loved the way that the bard used to seduce women. Perhaps this is indeed one of the most perfect models for us of the expected behavior that a gentleman should have.

# Conclusions

In this book we have talked about the figure of the gentleman and the lady. The truck driver and the street walker are metaphors that have been used to enlarge our understandings and to talk in a simple way (perhaps even naïve).

Modern men have access to many technological devices that didn't exist in ancient times. However, sexual manners can be seen as classic patterns of behavior that existed in the past, exist nowadays, and are suppose to exist in the future. This is the knowledge that this book tries to bring to you, reader. They weren't made up by the author, but taken from the lessons we learn when we see the way that actual ladies and gentlemen behave. They can tell us how to be one of them.

# *About the Author*

Marcellux Bosq is a non fiction writer and a visual artist.

He writes about self-help, psychology, technology and entertainment. You can see his work at http://marcellux.tripod.com.

He is also an admirer of those people who enjoy the pleasures of life (including sex, of course).

# *Index*

0-595-27683-0